Foods of Ireland

Barbara Sheen

KIDHAVEN PRESS
A part of Gale, Cengage Learning

GALE
CENGAGE Learning

Detroit • New York • San Francisco • New Haven, Conn • Waterville, Maine • London

GALE
CENGAGE Learning™

LIBRARY OF CONGRESS CATALOGING-IN-PUBLICATION DATA

Sheen, Barbara.
  Foods of Ireland / by Barbara Sheen.
    p. cm. -- (A taste of culture)
  Includes bibliographical references and index.
  ISBN 978-0-7377-5114-7 (hardcover)
  1. Cookery, Irish--Juvenile literature. 2. Ireland--Social life and customs--Juvenile literature. I. Title.
  TX717.5.S5174 2010
  641.59417--dc22

                                                              2010018791

Kidhaven Press
27500 Drake Rd.
Farmington Hills MI 48331

ISBN-13: 978-0-7377-5114-7
ISBN-10: 0-7377-5114-2

Printed in the United States of America
1 2 3 4 5 6 7 14 13 12 11 10

Printed by Bang Printing, Brainerd, MN, 1ˢᵗ Ptg., 09/2010

Contents

Basic Ingredients

For much of its history, Ireland was a poor nation ruled by England. Despite cattle and sheep thriving in its pastures, crops growing well in its cool damp climate, and edible sea creatures living in its coastal waters, Ireland's people struggled to survive.

A small group of wealthy Englishmen owned most of the land. Many of the Irish people were **tenant farmers** who leased small patches of land from the landowners. Because the landlords kept the best land for themselves, the tenant farmers wound up with hard-to-cultivate rocky soil that yielded barely enough food to stay alive.

There were times when food was scarce. Although

FOOD REGIONS OF IRELAND

UNITED KINGDOM

Atlantic Ocean

• Londonderry

NORTHERN IRELAND

Belfast •

IRELAND

Galway •

★ Dublin

Limerick •

Waterford •

Cork •

Fish	
Lobster	
Oysters	
Prawns	
Dairy	
Pork	
Beef	
Lamb	
Potatoes	
Grains	
Sugar Beet	

Atlantic Ocean

seafood was available, especially to those living on the coasts, it was not eaten on a daily basis. This is because seafood was associated with religious fast days. Out of necessity, the Irish people relied on dairy products, grains, and potatoes to help them stay alive.

Today, there is plenty of food for everyone in Ireland. Yet, dairy products, grains, and potatoes are still a vital part of the Irish people's diet. Over time, they have come to love these basic ingredients.

White Meats

The Irish developed their love for dairy products, which they call **white meats**, more than 2,000 years ago when the Celts, a group of people from Eastern Europe, settled in Ireland. The Celts were dairy farmers. Soon dairy farming and the production of milk products became an

Dairy products are an important part of the Irish diet, making dairy farming one of Ireland's biggest industries.

Two Irelands

From 1541 to 1921, Ireland was ruled by Great Britain. In 1916 Irish rebels revolted against British rule. This was the start of the Anglo-Irish War, which lasted until 1921, when a truce was declared and the Irish Free State was formed. The state did not become completely independent from Great Britain until 1937. In 1948 it changed its name to the Republic of Ireland. Its capital is Dublin.

Four counties in northeastern Ireland chose not to be part of the Irish Free State. They preferred to be ruled by Great Britain. They took the name Northern Ireland. Northern Ireland remains part of the British Empire. Its capital is Belfast.

The two nations have different monetary systems and governments. They share telecommunication and water systems, and field one Olympic team.

essential part of Irish life. By the fifth century, the Irish had become skilled in turning milk into cheese, cream, and butter. For many years, dairy products were the Irish people's main source of protein.

Dairy farming is still one of Ireland's largest industries. The Irish countryside is covered with green pastures where lush nutrient-rich grasses grow. These grasses give the milk of Irish cows a fresh creamy taste that the Irish love.

Milk is served with every meal. Thick spoonfuls of cream, the part of milk that contains the most fat, top many desserts. Irish cream, writer Martin Hughes says, "is a treat to behold. Rich, thick, luscious, and full of flavor."[1]

Buttermilk

Buttermilk is another Irish favorite. It is an essential ingredient in Irish cooking and baking. Despite its name, buttermilk does not contain butter. It instead is the thin liquid that is left after cream is churned into butter.

Thicker and more sour than whole milk, buttermilk is similar to drinkable yogurt in taste and texture. Irish cooks use it in breads, puddings, and potato dishes. It is also a popular beverage. In fact, ancient Irish laws required hosts to provide visitors with a cup of buttermilk.

Butter and Cheese

Cheese is another Irish staple. The Irish first started making cheese as a way to preserve milk. Many tenant farmers paid part of their rent in homemade cheese. Today, the Irish produce 65 different types of cheese.

Butter is even more important. The Irish eat more butter than any other people in Europe. No meal is served without it. The Irish slather it on bread and potatoes. They add it to sauces, vegetables, and porridges. It is a key ingredient in all Irish baked goods. Butter is so important to the Irish people that there is a butter museum in Cork, Ireland, dedicated to butter's history in Ireland.

Irish butter is famous throughout the world. Food

The Cork Butter Museum in Cork, Ireland, celebrates the importance of butter in Irish culture.

writer Colman Andrews describes it as "dense, creamy, and delicious [and] ... so rich and so full of flavor that you almost want to eat it with a spoon."[2]

Hearty Grains

Butter spread on bread, or topping a bowl of oatmeal, is a perfect accompaniment to two other Irish staples— oats and wheat. Monks, who came to Ireland from Europe about 1,500 years ago, brought the grains with them. Oats, in particular, thrived in Ireland's cool, moist climate. For many years Irish oatcakes were the most common bread in Ireland. Made with oatmeal,

Cheese Toast

Cheese toast is an easy and tasty Irish dish. It makes a good breakfast, lunch, or snack. White or wheat bread can be used.

Ingredients
2 slices whole wheat bread, buttered
1 egg, beaten
1 cup grated cheddar cheese
½ teaspoon grainy mustard
pinch salt and pepper

Directions
1. Preheat the oven to 400°F.
2. Mix the egg, cheese, mustard, salt, and pepper together in a bowl.
3. Put the bread, butter side down, on a baking dish.
4. Spread the cheese mixture on the bread.
5. Bake in the oven until the bread slices are golden brown and puffy, about 15 minutes.

Serves 2.

salt, and water, and cooked on a griddle, oat cakes are crunchy flat biscuits that look like rice cakes. They are delicious eaten hot with lots of butter, or they can be stored in an airtight container for long periods without spoiling. Many nineteenth century Irish immigrants on their way to America carried oatcakes on the long sea journey.

Irish soda bread, too, can contain oats, although wheat is more commonly featured. Soda bread gets its name from the baking soda in the dough, which, when

Oat cakes are crunchy biscuits that are cooked on a griddle.

Soda Bread

Soda bread can be made with white or wheat flour; it can be plain or contain raisins and caraway seeds, depending on the cook's preference. This recipe combines wheat and white flour and has raisins. Feel free to make substitutions.

Ingredients

1 cup whole wheat flour
2 ½ cups all-purpose flour
1 teaspoon baking soda
1 tablespoon baking powder
½ teaspoon salt

3 tablespoons sugar
2 cups raisins
1 egg, beaten
1 cup buttermilk
½ cup butter, softened

Directions

1. Preheat the oven to 375°F.
2. Combine the flour, baking soda, baking powder, salt, sugar, and raisins in a bowl and mix together.
3. Make a hole in the center of the mixture. Add the egg, butter, and buttermilk. Mix well.
4. Form the dough into a round. Put it on a greased and floured baking sheet. Cut an "X" on the top of the bread. Brush the top of the dough with some melted butter combined with buttermilk.
5. Bake until a fork placed in the bread comes out clean, about 60 minutes.

Makes one large round loaf.
Serves 8–12.

To maintain its freshness, soda bread is best eaten on the day it is baked.

combined with buttermilk, causes the bread to rise.

Soda bread is dense and hearty with a nutty, earthy flavor. It is usually round in shape with a cross cut on the top of the loaf. According to Irish legend, the cross lets fairies escape from the dough. In reality, it allows air to circulate through the bread, which helps it to rise. Because it dries out quickly, soda bread is usually eaten soon after baking. In the past, Irish cooks baked a fresh loaf every day. They made the bread on an iron skillet placed in a **peat**-fueled kitchen hearth or fireplace.

Today Irish cooks have modern ovens. Many buy the bread ready-made in bakeries. But, store-bought or freshly baked, eaten warm and spread with soft melting butter, the bread is delicious.

Porridge

For at least one-thousand years, porridge has been a favorite way for Irish cooks to use grains. Oatmeal, in particular, is very popular. It provides warmth and energy, making it a perfect way to start or end a damp Irish day. Irish oatmeal is made with steel-cut oats. This means the grain is cut with steel disks into only two or three pieces. This gives the oats a coarse, nutty texture.

The oats are cooked in water or milk, and topped with a spoonful of honey, a pat of butter, and a splash of cold milk, buttermilk, or cream. The results are hearty and hot. Author Joanne Asala recalls her first taste of Irish oatmeal: "It was late at night, cold, and rainy. . . . Our hostess . . . brought us each a bowl of steaming porridge. It was the best meal I've ever had."[3]

Traditional Irish Homes

Until the twentieth century, many Irish peasants lived in one-room cottages. These were made of stone and had thatched roofs made of dried straw. Every house had a chimney or a hole in the roof for smoke to escape.

Inside, the floors were made of dried earth. A fire fueled with peat heated the cottage and was used for cooking. Some cottages had a stone hearth or fireplace to contain the fire; some did not. A bastible, a large iron baking pot that hung over the fire, and an iron griddle were used for cooking.

Some families had beds, while others slept on straw mats. Shelves served as a dresser. Other furniture included a bin to store potatoes, wooden stools, and chairs made of straw. There were pegs on the door to hang outdoor clothes. The family pig also shared the house. Chickens roosted on the rafters.

Potatoes

Although the Irish have not been eating potatoes, or **praties**, as the Irish call them, as long as they have been eating porridge, potatoes play a very important role in the Irish diet, and in Irish history.

Potatoes originated in the South American country of Peru. The English adventurer Sir Walter Raleigh brought them to Ireland in 1588. They were easy to grow, required very little space, and yielded much more per acre than grain. A tiny plot produced enough potatoes to keep a large family well fed. This made potatoes a perfect crop for Ireland's tenant farmers. Within a century, potatoes served with butter and soda bread was the most common meal in Ireland. Potatoes became so important to the Irish that when fungus caused the potato crop to fail in the mid-nineteenth century about one million Irish people died of hunger. Another two million fled to America. This time in Irish history is known as the great **famine**.

The Irish have never lost their love for potatoes. Today, the average Irish person eats about 304 pounds (138kg) of potatoes annually. They boil them, fry them, steam them, and bake them. They mash them with butter and milk. They add them to soups, stews, and casseroles. According to Hughes, "Many of Ireland's most

famous dishes call for, or assume, the inclusion of potatoes. Irish stew would be soup without them, and bacon and cabbage minus the potatoes just wouldn't do."[4]

Most Irish recipes would not be the same without potatoes, milk

The Irish enjoy eating potatoes in many different forms. Potato farls, shown here, are similar to a potato pancake and are often served at breakfast.

products, and grains. Although modern Irish society is much different from Irish society in the past and the Irish no longer have to depend on these basic ingredients for survival, they still rely on these hearty staples, not because they have to, but because they enjoy the food.

2

Simple, Filling, and Flavorful

The Irish people's favorite dishes are simple, filling, and flavorful. They use readily available local ingredients. Irish stew, **rashers** and eggs, and potato dishes like **boxty**, **champ**, **colcannon**, and **Dublin coddle** are among the most popular.

Irish Stew

Irish stew is Ireland's most famous dish. Poor Irish peasants created the dish centuries ago as a way to use tough cuts of meat. Back then, the stew featured potatoes, onions, and goat meat or **mutton,** the meat of sheep more than eighteen months old. Most Irish tenant farmers did not own sheep. When the wealthy landowners slaughtered a sheep, they gave the tough-

Irish stew is one of Ireland's most well-known dishes. Although recipes for the stew can differ, it is always a warm, satisfying meal.

est parts of the animal, which they considered inedible, to their tenant farmers.

Male goat meat, too, often found its way into the stew. Unlike cows, sheep, or female goats, male goats did not provide the Irish people with milk or wool.

Consequently, the animals had little value and were often slaughtered for meat.

Both mutton and goat meat can be tough and chewy, especially if they are cooked quickly. But Irish cooks realized that cooking the meat slowly in Irish stew softened it. In fact, by the time the stew was ready to eat, the meat was fork-tender.

Irish Stew

Irish stew is not difficult to make, but it does take time. Beef can be substituted for lamb. The stew can be cooked in a slow cooker, such as a Crock-Pot, if the meat is browned first.

Ingredients

2 pounds lamb, cut into cubes
2 tablespoons vegetable oil
4 cups water or beef broth
1 large onion, sliced
3 large or 4 medium potatoes, peeled and cut into chunks
3 large carrots, peeled and cut into thick rounds
½ teaspoon pepper, thyme, salt
1 teaspoon fresh rosemary, chopped
2 tablespoons flour
3 tablespoons water

Directions

1. Heat the oil over medium heat in a large stockpot. Brown the lamb.
2. Remove two-thirds of the meat. Top the meat left in the pot with a third of the onions, followed by a third of the carrots, then a third of the potatoes. Sprinkle with salt, pepper, thyme, and rosemary. Repeat layering and seasoning two more times.
3. Pour the water or broth over the ingredients. Bring the stew to a boil. Reduce the heat to low, cooking for 1 1/2 to 2 hours, until all the ingredients are tender.
4. Mix the flour and 3 tablespoons water. Stir the mix into the stew to thicken it. Let it cook for 5 more minutes.
5. Serve in bowls. Top each bowl with a sprig of fresh parsley.

Serves 6.

Today lamb chops or pork ribs are more likely to be featured in Irish stew. Modern cooks also are apt to add leeks, parsley, butter, and carrots to the stewpot; although there is some controversy about carrots. Cooks in the south of Ireland say carrots give the stew color and sweetness, while those in the north insist that carrots ruin the flavor.

With or without carrots, the stew is easy to make and it is abundant. One pot can provide many meals. In fact, it is a tradition among Irish bachelors to make Irish stew on the weekend, then eat it throughout the

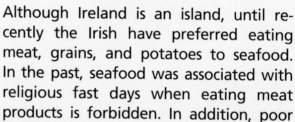

Seafood

Although Ireland is an island, until recently the Irish have preferred eating meat, grains, and potatoes to seafood. In the past, seafood was associated with religious fast days when eating meat products is forbidden. In addition, poor roads made it difficult for people living inland to get fresh seafood. Those living on the coasts, however, have always eaten seafood. Shellfish, like oysters, mussels, clams, cockles, and crabs, have a long history in Ireland. Archeologists have found piles of discarded oyster shells in coastal villages dating back to the Stone Age. In more recent times, it was a common sight to see Irish housewives buying live shellfish from local fishermen and carrying the shellfish home in buckets filled with seawater. The seawater was used for boiling unpeeled potatoes. Today seafood is popular throughout Ireland.

week. Served with soda bread, Irish stew is filling and flavorful. According to an article on Your Irish, a Web site dedicated to Irish culture, "There is no better meal than traditional Irish stew to heat up the body on a cold miserable day. . . . The ingredients are cheap to buy but the meal itself is one that will leave you stuffed for hours."[5]

Rashers and Eggs

Rashers and eggs, a big Irish breakfast, also known as a **fry-up**, is another hearty Irish favorite. Rashers are bits of cured pork similar in taste to American bacon. They are just one small part of this huge breakfast feast, which highlights pork products.

Since medieval times pork has been the most important meat in Ireland. Pigs are the only farm animals that

A big Irish breakfast, known as a fry-up, consists of (clockwise from bottom): fried eggs, bangers, tomato, black pudding, and rashers. Potatoes, toast, and other foods can be included, as well.

are native to Ireland. Most Irish tenant farmers owned a pig. Pigs are easy to raise because they do not require much land and can survive on potatoes, roots, or table scraps.

Farmers usually slaughtered one pig a year. Before the pig was slaughtered, it was fattened up. In order to preserve the meat, it was rubbed with salt, molasses, pepper, and saltpeter, a mineral that acts as a preservative. Then, it was dried and smoked over wood chips, juniper berries, and sod, which gave it an earthy, woodsy scent and flavor. The meat was stored by hanging it from the roof beams of Irish farmhouses where it could remain for months without spoiling.

Besides using pork for rashers, the Irish use it to make **bangers**, or sausage, another ingredient in

a fry-up. This huge meal, which is usually eaten on weekends due to time constraints, typically also includes two fried eggs, fried potatoes, fried tomatoes, fried mushrooms, buttered toast, **black pudding**, and **white pudding**, which, despite their names, are not actually puddings.

Black pudding is sausage mixed with pig's blood and other ingredients, which is then fried and eaten for breakfast.

White and black puddings are two types of sausage. The main ingredient in black pudding is pig's blood. It is mixed with chopped onions, bits of organ meat such as pig's heart and liver, pig fat, spices, flour, and oatmeal so that it forms a soft batter. The batter is poured through a funnel into a casing made from pig's intestines. The outside of the casing is brushed with pig's blood, which turns it black when it cooks. Finally, the sausage is boiled until the blood thickens. White pudding is made the same way but without the blood.

The Irish have been making black and white puddings for more than one-thousand years. Author Brid Mahon describes how it was done long ago:

> When they killed pigs they kept the intestines to make puddings. They washed them clear in a running stream and they were left to soak in spring water overnight. The casings were cut into fifteen-inch lengths, tied at one end. Salt, lard, oatmeal, finely chopped onions, spices, peppers, and cloves, together with a cup of flour were mixed with the pig's blood, which had been collected in a bucket. Each pudding was three-quarters filled and tied at the end. It was dropped in a pot half-filled with water . . . cooked for about an hour . . . allowed to cool, and divided amongst the neighbors. This was always done.[6]

The puddings are sliced into small rounds and fried

Irish Folklore

The Irish have a rich tradition of story-telling. Many Irish stories concern fairies. Irish tales recognize two types of fairies: troop fairies and solitary fairies. Troop fairies are beautiful little creatures that live in groups in golden palaces under bushes and circles of stones, known as fairy raths. These naturally occurring circles of stone can be found throughout Ireland. Farmers try not to disturb them because it is considered bad luck to hurt a fairy.

Solitary fairies live alone. There are many kinds of solitary fairies. Leprechauns are the most well known. All leprechauns are male. They are much bigger than troop fairies. Leprechauns make shoes and guard treasures. If a human catches a leprechaun and demands his treasure, the leprechaun must give it up. But this rarely happens.

before serving. Although black and white pudding may not sound appealing to some people, eating them as part of a fry-up is a long-standing and honored tradition in Ireland.

And Potatoes, Too

Rashers and eggs would not be complete without fried potatoes. Boxty, fried potato pancakes, is a famous Irish dish. Out of necessity, the dish was created at the start of the great famine as a way to use diseased potatoes that were too watery to boil. Irish cooks found that by putting the flesh of these potatoes into a cloth and

Colcannon, a mashed potato dish, is similar to champ except that cabbage or kale is added instead of green onions.

squeezing the water out, they could salvage enough potato pulp to mix with flour and shape into thin cakes.

Modern cooks no longer have to do this. They use plump healthy potatoes and a blender to create the batter for boxty. The fluffy, light cakes are usually served rolled, wrapped around a filling of rashers, cabbage, or applesauce.

Boxty is just one of many favorite potato dishes of the Irish. Potatoes are also the main attraction in Dublin coddle, champ, and colcannon. Dublin coddle is a simple stew that combines potatoes, onions, rashers, and sausage. It originated in Dublin, and got its name because the stew is simmered so slowly that the Irish say it is babied or "coddled." This type of slow cooking allows all the flavors to mix and mingle, and all the ingredients to become tender.

Champ and colcannon are two more potato specialties. Both are made with boiled potatoes mashed with milk. Chopped green onions are added to the mashed potatoes to make champ, a dish that is a special favorite in Northern Ireland. Cabbage or kale is added for colcannon. Both dishes are served in soup bowls. Before eating champ or colcannon, diners make a small hole in the center of the mashed potatoes, which they fill with a generous helping of butter. Then they mound the potatoes on top of the hole so that each bite is drenched in butter. The combination of moist creamy potatoes, sweet melted butter, and fresh greens is tasty and comforting.

Champ

Champ is easy to make. To make colcannon, substitute sliced cabbage or kale for the green onions.

Ingredients

6 large baking potatoes, peeled and cut into chunks
1 bunch of green onions (scallions) chopped
1 ½ cups milk
4 tablespoons butter
salt and pepper to taste

Directions

1. Put the potatoes in a pot, cover with water. Bring the water to a boil, cook until the potatoes are tender, about 15 minutes.
2. While the potatoes are cooking, put the scallions in a pot with the milk. On low heat, bring the milk to a boil.
3. Mash the potatoes. Put them in a bowl.
4. Pour the hot milk with the green onions into the potatoes. Mix well.
5. Make an indentation in the center of the potatoes. Put the butter into the indentation. Sprinkle with salt and pepper.

Serves 4.

Champ can be eaten as a side dish or as a meal by itself.

Author Monica Sheridan recalls her mother's champ: "I can well remember eating it when I was a child. The soft potato was scooped up with a spoon from the outer edges. It was then dipped into the well of butter at the center. How lovely it tasted."[7]

Champ, colcannon, boxty, Dublin coddle, Irish stew, and rashers and eggs all are simple, hearty, and delicious traditional dishes. It is no wonder they are Irish favorites.

It Is Tea Time

The Irish love tea. They take tea breaks three times a day. The first break, which is known as **elevenses**, occurs at 11 A.M. The second is held around 3 P.M. During these breaks, the Irish enjoy a cup of tea and a snack. High tea, which is held at 5 or 6 P.M., is the final tea break. It is the same as a light supper, but of course the meal is accompanied by tea. According to writer Brenda Hyde, the Irish "take their tea *very* seriously! You won't find a convention, work meeting, or other event that does not allow for a morning and afternoon tea break. . . . The rich and poor alike love tea time."[8]

The Emerald Isle

Ireland is called the Emerald Isle because it is so lush and green. It is the second-largest island in Europe. It has meadows, plains, mountains, tall cliffs, lakes, and a wild, rugged coastline.

About 15,000 years ago, glaciers covered Ireland. Today, peat bogs (swamps made up of decayed vegetation) dot much of Ireland. Some of the bogs formed when glacier lakes dried up. Others formed when ancient people destroyed Irish forests. For many years, the Irish harvested peat for fuel.

The first people to settle Ireland arrived around 6000 B.C. Since that time many groups have occupied Ireland, including the Vikings. They built settlements that later became important Irish cities.

Although Ireland was once the poorest country in Europe, it is now one of the wealthiest. This is mainly due to the growth of high-tech industries. English and Gaelic are spoken in Ireland.

A Favorite Drink

The Irish drink more tea per person than any other group in the world. Ireland imports over 10,000 tons of tea each year. This amounts to four to six cups of tea per person per day.

Tea originated in Asia. The English brought it to Ireland in 1835. At first, it was too expensive for the average person to purchase. Over time, the price declined. By the end of the eighteenth century, tea had become

Tea breaks are a regular part of each day in Ireland.

Irish Tea

The Irish are particular about their tea. To make tea most like what is served in Ireland, use Irish breakfast tea available in supermarkets. Use a teapot to steep the tea bag in.

Ingredients
3 Irish breakfast tea bags
3 cups water
½ cup milk or cream
sugar to taste

Directions
1. Fill a teakettle with the water. Bring the water to a boil.
2. Pour 1 cup of water into the teapot, swirl it around to warm the teapot, then pour it out.
3. Put the tea bags in the teapot. Add the remaining water. Put the lid on the teapot. Cover the teapot with a clean dish towel. Let the tea steep for five minutes.
4. Divide the milk between two cups. Fill the cups with tea. Add sugar to taste. Stir well.

Enjoy with cookies or cake. Serves 2.

When boiling water for tea, it is best to heat it over the stove rather than heat it in a microwave.

popular with everyone. Traveling salesmen, known as tea men, went door-to-door selling tea, and little stores where people could exchange cheese or butter for tea opened up throughout Ireland.

Sharing tea is an Irish tradition. It is always offered to guests in Irish homes, and it is the Irish people's favorite snack. Stopping whatever one is doing for a tea break gives the Irish a chance to relax and unwind while they visit with friends.

Not just any tea will do. The Irish are very particular about their tea. They prefer black tea from Kenya. It is much stronger and more full-bodied than the tea Americans are used to. According to Hughes, "If you're used to 'drawing' your teabag [letting the tea bag sit in the boiled water] for three minutes or so, a quick dip with an Irish bag will have the desired effect. The real thing is altogether much stronger—so strong you reckon a spoon could stand up in it."[9]

To make tea, Irish cooks fill a kettle with fresh water. They never re-boil water. Doing so, they say, ruins the taste of the tea. The kettle is heated until the water boils. The water is poured into a teapot along with one tea bag per person, plus one extra tea bag for the pot. The tea is left to steep for about five minutes. A special cover known as a tea cozy is put over the teapot to keep it warm.

When the tea is ready, one person acts as the "mother." He or she pours tea into everyone's cup. Because the tea is so strong, it is usually taken with milk and sugar.

Scones

Scones, pastries similar to American biscuits, are a popular accompaniment to tea. Scones originated in the sixteenth century in Scotland and quickly became popular in England, Wales, and Ireland. Back then, scones were made of oats and cooked on a griddle.

Modern scones are a type of **quick bread**. They are made with flour, baking soda, butter, eggs, sugar, and

Scones pair well with jam, butter, clotted cream and, of course, tea.

milk or buttermilk, and are baked in an oven. They may contain raisins or currants, which are golden raisins, or they may be plain. Many Irish bakers glaze the top with a bit of sugar.

Irish scones are not overly sweet. They are light, moist, and flaky with a hint of sweetness. The Irish can hardly resist them served warm, topped with butter, fresh jam, or rich, thick cream. "Scones with their sweet sugary tops are still one of my favorite things in the whole world," says Irish chef Darina Allen. "When I was a child, our enormous family of nine regularly polished off a tray of them after school."[10]

Apple Treats

A variety of treats made with apples is another popular accompaniment to tea, in addition to being a well-liked dessert. Monks planted the first apple trees in Ireland about 1,500 years ago. Apples have been growing there ever since. There are familiar apples like Granny Smith and Golden Delicious, as well as heirloom, or old varieties such as Beauty of Bath, a sweet apple with pink flesh.

Irish cooks make dozens of different apple dishes such as apple pie, apple crumble, apple tarts, applesauce, and apple dumplings, to name just a few. Parents have been passing down their apple recipes to their children for centuries. Irish apple cake is a traditional treat that has been popular for many years. It can be made with almost any variety of apples. It is especially popular in autumn when Irish bakers use freshly

Apples grow abundantly in Ireland. As a result, apple desserts, such as this apple and oatmeal cake, are a favorite among the Irish.

picked apples in the cake.

This simple cake is made with apples, flour, butter, eggs, milk, sugar, cinnamon, and nutmeg. It is a moist, gently spiced cake with a crunchy top and a mouth-watering fragrance. Served warm and topped with a dollop of chilled cream, it is, according to Allen, "the traditional dessert in Ireland."[11]

Pratie apple cake is another favorite. It is more like a tart or a little pie than a cake. To make it, bakers sandwich sliced apples, butter, and sugar between dough made of mashed potatoes, butter, and flour. The cake

Apple Crumble

This is an easy-to-make Irish apple treat.

Ingredients
4 medium apples, peeled, cored, and chopped
⅝ cup flour
½ cup granulated (white) sugar
¼ cup brown sugar
½ cup butter
1 teaspoon cinnamon
½ teaspoon salt

Directions
1. Preheat oven to 350°F.
2. Lightly butter a baking pan or casserole dish. Put the apples in the pan.
3. Combine the brown sugar and cinnamon. Sprinkle it on top of the apples.
4. Combine the flour, granulated sugar, and salt in a bowl. Cut in the butter. Mix until pea-like crumbs form.
5. Sprinkle the flour mixture on top of the apples. Bake until the top is crunchy and the apples are soft, 40 to 45 minutes.
6. Let the crumble cool for a few minutes before serving.

Serves 4–6. Top with thick cream or vanilla ice cream.

Apple crumble is a tasty, easy-to-make treat.

Wild Plants

Foraging, or gathering of, wild plants has always been popular in Ireland. Wild garlic, wild cabbage, and nettles are gathered in the spring. Nettles are herbs covered with tiny hairs that sting when touched. The stingers deactivate when the plant is cooked. The Irish use nettle leaves to make nettle soup, which also contains potatoes, onions, and milk.

Foragers also gather dulse, a type of seaweed, which is often added to soups, stews, and mashed potatoes. Carrageen moss, another sea plant, is gathered off rocks. It contains agar-agar, a type of gelatin that is used as a thickening agent in ice cream and puddings.

Wild strawberries, blueberries, blackberries, elderberries, and plums are gathered in the autumn. They are eaten fresh and used to make jams and jellies. Hazelnuts are also gathered in the fall. The Irish use them in breads, cakes, and puddings.

Nettle leaves and vegetables are being prepared to make nettle soup.

is typically cooked on a griddle until it is golden brown. As it heats, the apples soften, and the butter and sugar in the filling melt and blend.

The cake is usually served piping hot, drizzled with honey, or fresh cream. It is "the high point of many a farmhouse high tea, especially when using home-grown apples,"[12] says authors Biddy White Lennon and Georgina Campbell.

Gurr Cakes

Gurr cakes are another traditional and popular sweet treat. Also known as fruit slices, these tasty pastries are a clever combination of day-old cake or bread and dried fruit.

A thrifty nineteenth-century Dublin baker invented gurr cake as a way to use stale cake and bread that would otherwise go to waste. To make it, bakers combine bits of stale bread or day-old cake with sugar, warm milk, butter, eggs, and dried fruit. The mixture is sandwiched between pastry dough and baked until the dough is golden. The top of the cake is sprinkled with sugar; then the cake is cut into little squares, which were sold for a halfpenny each in the nineteenth century.

Because the little cakes were the cheapest item in the bakery, they were very popular with children, especially those "on the gurr," Irish slang for students who were skipping school. It is likely that the cake got its name because of its popularity with these children. An article on the Austerity Kitchen, a Web site about thrifty cooking, insists, "you need not be dodging school in order to enjoy a piece of this delightfully frugal [inexpensive] cake. . . . Enjoy it with tea, coffee, or a glass of warm . . . milk."[13]

Gurr cake does go well with a cup of tea. So do scones and apple treats. Taking a tea break gives the Irish a chance to relax while enjoying a steaming cup of their favorite beverage. And, when it is accompanied by a flaky scone topped with thick rich cream, a fragrant slice of apple cake made with freshly picked apples, or a square of sweet, fruity gurr cake, tea time becomes even more pleasurable.

Let's Celebrate

Irish holidays are celebrated with special food traditionally associated with the day. Barmbrack, Christmas cake, pancakes, and cabbage and bacon are among these special dishes.

Halloween Treats

The Irish have been celebrating Halloween in one form or another for about 2,000 years. The ancient Celts called the holiday **Samhain** (SAH-win), meaning summer's end. They believed that on Samhain the barrier between the natural world and the world of the supernatural disappeared, allowing humans to encounter ghosts and fairies, and to foretell the future with more ease.

Small charms, each with their own meaning, are baked inside of barmbrack bread each Halloween. Those eating the bread have fun discovering which object is baked in their piece.

Even today, the Irish have fun fortune-telling on Halloween. Barmbrack helps them to do so. It is one of only a few Irish pastries made with yeast. Barmbrack, which means speckled yeast cake, is a light, sweet bread flavored with cinnamon, nutmeg, allspice, cloves, and brown sugar and filled with dried fruit.

What makes it a Halloween favorite is the various objects that are wrapped up and baked inside it. Each object symbolizes something different and is used to foretell the future. For instance, there is a ring, which symbolizes marriage, a coin for wealth, a pea for poverty, a matchstick for travel, and so on.

Traditionally, finding a particular object in a slice of the cake foretells what will happen to the finder in the upcoming year. Darina Allen recalls that in her childhood "everyone longed for the ring which meant certain marriage before the year ended, even if you were only five!"[14]

Christmas Cake

Christmas is another holiday when traditional foods are eaten. In the past, goose was often the main course for Christmas dinner. Today, turkey stuffed with sausage is more likely to be served. No matter the main course, it is the Christmas cake that is the high point of the meal.

Although many modern cooks buy the cake ready-made, traditionally, Irish bakers start preparing the cake shortly after Halloween. To taste its best Irish Christmas cake, which is similar to fruitcake, needs to age.

It is a rich cake packed with dried and candied fruit, almonds, butter, brown sugar, spices, and Irish whiskey, which serves to moisten the cake and plump up the fruit. As the cake ages, the alcohol in the whiskey evaporates so it does not have any effect on those eating it.

Christmas cake is a holiday tradition in Ireland.

The Irish have been eating Christmas cake for about a thousand years. In the past, many Irish families scrimped and saved to purchase the exotic ingredients that go into the cake. Ingredients like ginger, sugar-coated cherries, and candied citrus peels all were imported from the Middle East, and were, therefore, expensive especially since a Christmas cake can weigh up to 10 pounds (4.54kg).

Customarily, making the cake is a family event. Even young children help. In many families it is a Christmas tradition for each member to make a wish as they stir the batter. Allen recalls, "In our family there was no shortage of eager helpers. As children stoned the muscatel raisins, washed and halved the jewel-like cherries, diced the chunks of candied peel and citron and even helped with the laborious creaming of butter and soft dark brown sugar."[15]

Cake Dances

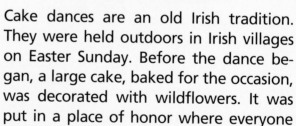

Cake dances are an old Irish tradition. They were held outdoors in Irish villages on Easter Sunday. Before the dance began, a large cake, baked for the occasion, was decorated with wildflowers. It was put in a place of honor where everyone could see it. Then local musicians started playing music. Everyone would dance. The couple that danced for the longest time was said to "take the cake." They were given the cake, which they sliced up and shared with everyone at the dance.

Once the cake is baked, it is placed in a cool spot to age. Right before Christmas, it is frosted with **marzipan**, a sweet paste made of almonds and sugar that stiffens to the consistency of hard candy when it dries. The hardened marzipan is covered with a white icing to make a snow scene. Christmas decorations such as little plastic Christmas trees may also decorate the cake, which is set out in a place of honor before Christmas Day.

Eaten for dessert on Christmas day, the cake is not as sweet or as dense as a typical fruitcake. It is spicier, and more fragrant and moist, making it a perfect Christmas treat.

Pancake Tuesday

Food is so important to Irish holiday celebrations that one holiday, Pancake Tuesday, is named for the food associated with it. Pancake Tuesday falls on the day before Lent, a forty-day period prior to Easter in which many Irish people give up meat, eggs, and dairy products for religious reasons. Pancakes slathered with butter are traditionally eaten before this fast begins. This practice dates back to the Middle Ages. It started as a way to use up eggs, milk, and butter, preventing temptation during Lent.

The Irish make pancakes with lots of whole milk, unsalted butter, and eggs. They cook them on one side until they are golden. Then, they flip the cakes. This involves tossing the pancakes high into the air so that they turn over, then catching them in the pan.

Flipping the pancakes takes skill. In fact, accord-

The day before Lent is Pancake Tuesday in Ireland. Besides eating the delicious cakes, tradition calls for the cook to flip the pancakes high into the air while cooking them.

ing to Irish tradition, if an unmarried woman tosses a pancake and catches it in the pan on Pancake Tuesday, she will be married within a year. If the pancake does not turn or she drops it, she will remain single. Today, many Irish communities hold pancake races on Pancake Tuesday in which local women carrying pans race to a finish line tossing pancakes as they run.

It is not just Irish women who are skilled at pancake tossing. Writer Bridget Haggerty recalls her father's ability: "We all watched as he mixed the ingredients, prepared the pan, and then poured the batter for the first cake. Then, we'd let out loud whoops of glee as he deftly tossed the cake high into the air. Everyone held their breath to see if he'd catch it back into the pan again. Rarely did he miss."[16]

The pancakes are eaten right out of the pan, crowned with melted butter, a sprinkle of sugar, and a squirt of lemon. They are thin, light, and buttery.

Buttermilk Pancakes

These are easy to make. They can be cooked on a griddle or in a frying pan.

Ingredients
1 ¼ cup flour
1 egg
1 ¼ cup buttermilk
1 teaspoon baking soda
2 tablespoons sugar
¼ cup melted butter

Directions
1. Combine the dry ingredients and mix well.
2. Add the buttermilk, butter, and egg. Stir to make a thick but pourable batter. Do not over stir. The batter can have lumps.
3. Coat a large frying pan with nonstick cooking spray. Heat the pan over medium heat. Drop spoonfuls of the batter into the pan. Cook for 2 to 3 minutes on one side until the edges harden and/or the bubbles burst. Turn the pancakes over and cook on both sides.

Serves 4.

When making pancakes, the cook can decide how large or small to make each cake.

Celebrating Saint Patrick's Day

Special foods are also associated with Saint Patrick's Day, which is probably the most famous of all Irish holidays. It is both a religious and national holiday in Ireland. The Irish celebrate on March 17 by going to church to honor Saint Patrick, and by pinning a **shamrock** to their clothes. It is a three-leaf clover that represents the Christian Holy Trinity of the Father, Son, and Holy Spirit. Towns and cities hold parades. Families get together for dinner. Some people go to neighborhood bars known as pubs. Pubs are popular social meeting places. There they have a pint of Irish beer and a bite to eat. Both at home and in pubs, cabbage and bacon, a stew featuring pork and cabbage, is most likely to be served.

Unlike in America, the Irish call every part of the pig, except the legs, bacon. The meat used to make cabbage and bacon is more likely to be pork shoulder than American-style bacon. To make the dish, Irish cooks slowly boil the meat in water for about two hours. Fifteen minutes before the meat is done, cabbage is added to the water. The cabbage, which is cooked until it is soft, picks up the smoky, salty flavor of the meat. Served alongside the meat, the cabbage is topped with a lump of butter and a sprinkle of white pepper. Potatoes almost always accompany the dish.

Cabbage and bacon tastes somewhat like American corned beef and cabbage. Interestingly, nineteenth century Irish immigrants in the United States

Bacon and cabbage is always served on Saint Patrick's Day in Ireland.

tried to make Irish-style cabbage and bacon in their new homes. Because of different smoking and curing methods, American pork did not taste like Irish bacon. Salted, or corned, beef, however, was more similar to Irish bacon, so Irish immigrants substituted corned beef for Irish bacon. Over time, corned beef and cabbage became associated with Ireland and Saint Patrick's Day in America. In truth, corned beef and cabbage is an American dish. It is not often eaten in Ireland. Nothing can replace cabbage and bacon there.

Indeed, when it comes to celebrating special days

Spring Lamb

Raising sheep for wool and meat is a big industry in Ireland. Most Irish sheep roam in flocks on Irish hillsides and meadows. They are not kept penned up or fed grain or chemicals. They feed on rich grasses, wildflowers, and herbs, which gives their meat a sweet, delicate flavor.

Lambs are usually born in the early spring. They are slaughtered right before Easter when they are still quite young. Because they are young, their meat is especially tender.

Traditionally, roast leg of lamb is served on Easter Sunday in Ireland. The meat is rubbed with butter and seasoned with salt and pepper, then slowly roasted in the oven with carrots and onions. It is served with gravy, mint jelly, and sauce made with milk, butter, flour, and parsley. Peas, potatoes, and crusty Irish bread are popular accompaniments.

Bacon and Cabbage

Try making bacon and cabbage for Saint Patrick's Day. It is usually served with boiled potatoes.

Ingredients
2–3 pounds pork shoulder
1 head of cabbage, outer leaves removed, cut
     into quarters
1 tablespoon butter
salt and pepper to taste

Directions
1. Put the pork in a large pot. Cover with water. Bring the water to a boil. Lower the heat to medium low. Cook the pork for about 30 minutes per pound plus an extra 30 minutes, 1 ½ hours for two pounds, 2 hours for three pounds, etc. As the meat cooks, skim off the foam.
2. About 15 minutes before the meat is cooked, add the cabbage to the pot. Cook 20 minutes. Continue cooking until the pork is fully cooked throughout and the cabbage is soft.
3. Remove the pork from the pot. Cut it into thick slices.
4. Remove the cabbage from the pot. Drain it. Put the cabbage on a plate. Season with salt and pepper to taste. Top with the butter.

Serve with boiled potatoes, bread, and grainy mustard.
Serves 4–6.

there is no substitute for cabbage and bacon, pancakes, Christmas cake, and barmbrack in Ireland. These foods play an important part in Irish life and culture. Without them, Irish holidays would not be as much fun or as memorable.

Metric Conversions

Mass (weight)

1 ounce (oz.)	= 28.0 grams (g)
8 ounces	= 227.0 grams
1 pound (lb.)	
or 16 ounces	= 0.45 kilograms (kg)
2.2 pounds	= 1.0 kilogram

Liquid Volume

1 teaspoon (tsp.)	= 5.0 milliliters (ml)
1 tablespoon (tbsp.)	= 15.0 milliliters
1 fluid ounce (oz.)	= 30.0 milliliters
1 cup (c.)	= 240 milliliters
1 pint (pt.)	= 480 milliliters
1 quart (qt.)	= 0.96 liters (l)
1 gallon (gal.)	= 3.84 liters

Pan Sizes

8- inch cake pan	= 20 x 4-centimeter cake pan
9-inch cake pan	= 23 x 3.5-centimeter cake pan
11 x 7-inch baking pan	= 28 x 18-centimeter baking pan
13 x 9-inch baking pan	= 32.5 x 23-centimeter baking pan
9 x 5-inch loaf pan	= 23 x 13-centimeter loaf pan
2-quart casserole	= 2-liter casserole

Temperature

212° F	= 100° C (boiling point of water)
225° F	= 110° C
250° F	= 120° C
275° F	= 135° C
300° F	= 150° C
325° F	= 160° C
350° F	= 180° C
375° F	= 190° C
400° F	= 200° C

Length

1/4 inch (in.)	= 0.6 centimeters (cm)
1/2 inch	= 1.25 centimeters
1 inch	= 2.5 centimeters

Notes

Chapter 1: Basic Ingredients

1. Martin Hughes, *World Food: Ireland*. Victoria, Australia: Lonely Planet, 2000, p. 63.

2. Colman Andrews, "Ireland from Farm to Fork," *Saveur*, March 2006, p. 55.

3. Joan Asala, *Celtic Folklore Cooking*. Woodbury, MN: Llewellyn, 2009, p. 72.

4. Hughes, *World Food: Ireland*, p. 35.

Chapter 2: Simple, Filling, and Flavorful

5. "Traditional Irish Stew Recipe," Your Irish.com. www.yourirish .com/irish-stew.htm.

6. Brid Mahon, *Land of Milk and Honey: The Story of Traditional Irish Food and Drink*. Cork, Ireland: Mercier Press, 1998, p. 59.

7. Monica Sheridan, *The Art of Irish Cooking*. New York: Gramercy, 1975, p. 103.

Chapter 3: It Is Tea Time

8. Brenda Hyde, "Irish Tea Traditions," Old Fashioned Living. http://oldfashionedliving.com/irishtea/html.

9. Hughes, *World Food Ireland*, p. 148.

10. Darina Allen, *Irish Traditional Cooking*. London: Kyle Books, 2005, p. 227.

11. Allen, *Irish Traditional Cooking*, p. 193.

12. Biddy White Lennon and Georgina Campbell, *The Irish Heritage Cookbook*. London: Lorenz Books, 2007, p. 217.

13. "Gurr Cake," October 21, 2009, *The Austerity Kitchen*. www .theausteritykitchen.com/2009/10/gurr-cake.html.

Chapter 4: Let's Celebrate

14. Quoted in "Hallowe'en Barmbrack," Catholic Culture.org, www.catholicculture.org/culture/liturgicalyear/recipes/view.cfm?id=1335.

15. Allen, *Irish Traditional Cooking.* p. 244

16. Bridget Haggerty, "Shrove Tuesday Pancakes!" *Iris Culture and Customs.* www.irishcultureandcustoms.com/ACalend/ShroveTues.html.

Glossary

bangers: The Irish term for sausages.

barmbrack: Sweet bread eaten on Halloween.

black pudding: Sausage made with pig's blood.

boxty: A type of potato pancake.

buttermilk: The liquid that remains when milk is churned into butter.

champ: Potatoes mashed with green onions and butter.

colcannon: Potatoes mashed with butter and cabbage or kale.

Dublin coddle: A potato stew.

elevenses: An 11 A.M. tea break.

famine: A time of widespread food shortage.

fry-up: A large Irish breakfast featuring different fried foods.

gurr cakes: Pastries made with stale bread or cake and dried fruit.

marzipan: A sweet paste made of almonds and sugar.

mutton: The meat of an adult sheep.

peat: Decayed grass, moss, and other organic matter

that can be dried and used for fuel.

porridges: Dishes made by boiling grains in milk or water.

praties: The Irish name for potatoes.

quick bread: Bread made without yeast.

rashers: The Irish name for salted and cured pork similar to bacon.

Samhain: An ancient Celtic celebration similar to Halloween.

shamrock: A three-leaf clover worn on Saint Patrick's Day.

steel-cut oats: Oat grain used in oatmeal that is cut by steel disks into two or three pieces.

tenant farmers: People who live on and farm rented land, paying the owner with money or farm products.

white meats: The name the Irish use for dairy products.

white pudding: Sausage made with pork organ meat, spices, and grain.

Books

Robert Bowden and Ronan Foley, *Focus on Ireland*. Strongsville: OH, 2007. Looks at Ireland's history, government, people, economy, geography, and culture with maps.

Feargal Brougham and Caroline Farrell, *The Great Famine*. London: Evans Brothers, 2008. Discusses the Irish potato famine and its effect on Ireland.

Duncan Crosbie, *Professor Murphy's History of Ireland*. Dublin: Gill and Macmillan, 2009. Guided by a cartoon figure, the book looks at Irish history with lots of colored illustrations.

Brendan O'Brien, *The Story of Ireland*. Dublin: O'Brien Press, 2007. A fun book with humorous illustrations and lots of information about Irish history.

Web Sites

Fact Monster, "Ireland," (http://www.factmonster .com/ipka/A0107648.html). Facts on Irish geography, history, government, and current challenges, with a map and flag.

Kool Kidz of Ireland (http://homepage.eircom

.net/~whitechurchns/kool_kidz_of_ireland.htm). This Web site was created by Irish children. It has information about Irish culture, food, geography, favorite sports, and links to contact the children.

National Geographic Kids, "Ireland," (www.national geographic.com/Places/Find/Ireland). Provides facts, photos, a map, video, and an e-card on Ireland.

Time for Kids, "Ireland," (http://www.time forkids.com/TFK/teachers/aw/wr/article/ 0,28138,1721689,00.html). This Web site gives a sightseeing tour of Ireland with links to a time line, fact file, an e-card, and other information.

Index

Picture Credits

Cover Photo: Image copyright Monkey Business Images, 2010. Used under license from Shutterstock.com.

© Bill Bachmann/Alamy, 6

© Bon Appetit/Alamy, 22, 25, 34, 49

Image copyright Paul Cowan, 2010. Used under license from Shutterstock.com., 12

© Food Features/Alamy, 37

© foodfolio/Alamy, 18, 31, 43

Gale, Cengage Learning, 5

© The Daniel Heighton Food Collection/Alamy, 32

© Tim Hill/Alamy, 36

© Marshall Ikonography/Alamy, 11

© Robert Judges/Alamy, 46

© mediablitzimages (uk) Limited/Alamy, 42

Image copyright Monkey Business Images, 2010. Used under license from Shutterstock.com., 15, 27

© keith morris/Alamy, 47

© Neil Setchfield/Alamy, 9

© Jim Wileman/Alamy, 38

© Yetish Yetish/Alamy, 21

About the Author

Barbara Sheen is the author of more than 50 books for young people. She lives in New Mexico with her family. In her spare time, she likes to swim, walk, garden, and read. Of course, she loves to cook!